TIPS, TRICKS AND INSIGHT FOR SURVIVING YOUR KITCHEN REMODEL

A step-by-step guide to planning and managing a successful kitchen remodel

Kyle & Sandy McNatt

Tips, Tricks and Insight For Surviving Your Kitchen Remodel
ISBN: 978-1501062582
Published by Adventure Publishing Services
info@adventurepublishingservices.com

A FREE GIFT FOR YOU

To express my thanks for your purchase we would like to give you a free gift. Follow the link below and you can download a Week of Easy Dinner Recipes you can make with only a crockpot and an electric frying pan PLUS a list of critical questions you should ask your contractor before you hire him.

Go to the link below to receive your FREE forms
Click here for your FREE Forms.

We know these will be helpful to you in your quest for your dream kitchen!
Thank you!
Kyle and Sandra McNatt

Contents

Introduction: Kitchen Remodeling

Do you love your house but are tired of your old outdated kitchen? Maybe you just bought a great place in an awesome location but want to put your own style into the most central part of your home, the kitchen. If you have so much as even toyed with the thought of remodeling your kitchen, this book is for you.

It might seem like a mammoth task, and to be honest it is. Remodeling does require a lot of attention to detail but with a plan and the great advice in this book you can survive and even enjoy the transformation taking place in your home. Here we will help you find the style you like, set a budget, hire a qualified contractor and successfully manage your kitchen remodel from start to finish.

Without a plan and a great contractor these projects can go south quickly. Don't let your dream project become your worst nightmare. Be proactive and prepared, learn how to avoid conflicts with your contractor and remain living comfortably in your home during construction.

With the information provided in this book you will have the tools you need to make the decisions you need and get the kitchen you have always dreamed of.

Chapter 1: Why remodel?

Why remodel? That is an excellent question. Knowing all of the reasons why you want to remodel will help you focus your project and get exactly what you are looking for in your new kitchen.

Here are a number of good reasons why you should remodel. Think about which apply to your kitchen.

- Fresh Look– Think about it. Where do your friends and family gather in your home? Usually gatherings center around the kitchen. People talk, mingle and eat here. An updated kitchen will make a great impression on your guests. We spend so much time in our kitchen areas so it makes sense that this area should be someplace we are happy and comfortable.

- New Home – Location, location, location is really the key to a great home. Because of this, many people will buy homes that need a little work or updating. If you bought your home for its great location but don't like the kitchen, now is the time to put your own unique touch on the house by updating. The kitchen is the most central part of your home so start here then carry the color scheme and style you choose on to other areas of your home.

- Increasing the value of your home – Money Magazine has ranked kitchen remodeling as the best return on investment you can make in your home. You can expect up to 10 to 15% appreciation in value of your entire home just by remodeling your kitchen. An investment with instant returns like this cannot be ignored.

- Selling your home- When you look at sales listings you will notice that a kitchen remodel is one of the first things real estate agents bring to your attention. If you are thinking of selling even a few years from now, talk to your real estate agent about updates that will increase your home value almost dollar for dollar. Besides getting top dollar for that remodel you will also sell your home faster, which means less hassle for you, another giant bonus.

- Reduce your footprint – You might choose to remodel your kitchen so that you can add energy efficient appliances and plan the new layout to allow natural sunlight to enter. Sometimes there are even government programs that offer rebates for use of energy efficient appliances and those that run on alternative source of energy. So you do your part in saving the environment while at the same time you are saving money on your utility bills. There could be no better way to reduce your carbon footprint than making your home more energy efficient.

- Make your Kitchen User Friendly – Today's modern kitchens have a lot of unique ways to increase your useable storage space. Take advantage of these features to make your kitchen easier to use. A kitchen that is inviting, friendly, and has easy accessibility will get used more. Eating at home is healthier and will save you a lot of money in the long run. So remodeling that old, ugly space can have a positive impact on your family's health and budget as well.

- As seen on TV – You may also want to remodel your kitchen after being inspired by ones you saw on TV. Home improvement shows are very interesting and teach you how to do things around your home with simplicity. If you have always wanted that kitchen you saw on TV, it is time you get it done.

As you can see there are lots of really good reasons to remodel a kitchen. So now that we understand the why, we move to the how, and the how is all about planning. The better we plan, the better we will execute. This will include a better set of expectations, a more accurate budget, a real vision of what we want, and rock solid roadmap to make it a reality.

Chapter 2: Planning Your Dream Kitchen

So what does your dream kitchen look like? Do you know exactly what you want? Or, do you need to do some exploring? Even if you think you know what you want it is a good idea to go out and look at what is available before you make a final decision.

A new kitchen is a significant investment so take some time to decide exactly what you want and need. Sometimes, to balance our budget we need to make some adjustment in want verses what we need, but that is okay. In the end, with careful planning you will have a kitchen you will love spending time in no matter what your budget.

Start your plan by really taking time to look around your existing kitchen. Make a list of all of the features that you like. Maybe you love the way it is laid out. Maybe you love the pantry access or maybe your favorite part is the view out the window. List everything you like about the current kitchen so you keep these features in the new kitchen.

Now make a list of all of the things you dislike about your kitchen. Do you want to change the color scheme? Is it to dark and you need to add additional lighting or bring in more natural light? Is the stove in an awkward location? Do you love the cabinets but hate the countertops? Maybe you want to add an island to create additional workspace and provide a place for guests to sit when you are entertaining.

Here is an example of one of our kitchen remodel lists:

What we want to keep in our kitchen:
1. Kitchen layout is great.
2. Efficient work triangle.
3. Great natural lighting from windows.
4. Appliances in great shape and already matching.

What we want to change in our kitchen:
1. New cabinets – old, outdated.
2. Replace laminate tops with modern stone product
3. New flooring to replace outdated tile (wood?)
4. Increase lighting at night (under cabinet lighting?)
5. Bring modern, classic look into the home

Now you have a place to start planning your new kitchen. I can tell you that moving walls, appliances or the water source in your kitchen can significantly increase the price of your remodel, but sometimes these moves are necessary to create a kitchen that is truly functional or a work of art.

If these moves are important, you will find a way to work them into your final budget. However, it is good to have a backup plan, though in the event they prove too cost prohibitive. If necessary, a good designer can help you work around these issues so don't dismay.

So where can we look for inspiration for our new kitchen design?

Start on the internet

With the internet, amazing kitchen designs and ideas are just a few clicks away. A great way to start is to find and bookmark pictures of kitchens you like. If you are married or have a significant other, look at kitchens separately. Then, when you have a collection of about 10 or so examples that you like, share them with your significant other to see if they also feel the same way about them. Ideally, you will both like at least some of the same designs, features or color concepts.

Open up a Google or Bing search and search for terms like "kitchen remodel pictures" or even just "kitchen remodel" and then at the top of the search page choose Images. Suddenly you will have hundreds of pictures to choose from. If you know the style of kitchen you want then you can add that to the search as well. Examples of this might be "modern kitchen remodel" or "country kitchen remodel"

TV show and company websites are another good way to find pictures. Although they will probably come up in the search engine search by looking at websites like HDTV, Home Depot, Lowes, kitchen and bath contractors, designers, etc. you will find lots of pictures that have been categorized and sometimes they will have costs associated with the pictures.

Another way to find kitchen pictures is with social networking sites like Facebook and Pinterest. Excited homeowners around the world like to share their kitchen remodeling projects. Websites like Pinterest are a great place to find inspiration. In fact, Pinterest can be a fantastic source as users create specific boards to which they pin images and visual plans for projects. A simple search will provide access to boards, which were created by homeowners while planning for their remodeling projects. If you want you can create a board here too and share it with others to get their opinions as well.

YouTube is another great source for inspiration. There are a number of video tutorials created by experts and amateurs alike on kitchen remodeling projects. You can view these videos and gain valuable ideas and insights from experts in kitchen remodeling. These tutorials are easy to follow as they have been designed for homeowners remodeling for the first time. You will also find links to resources that can help you plan your project.

Remodeling forums are another source that provides an interactive community. You can speak with experts and homeowners who have remodeled their kitchen. Most users on these forums are very helpful and all you need to do is ask. They also have dedicated photo gallery sections that you can browse. We highly recommend forums as a source of inspiration for remodeling ideas.

Magazines & Books

There are several magazines dedicated to home improvement and specifically kitchen design. Kitchens, Beautiful Kitchens, Kitchens & Bath are just a few of these currently available. Look for them online or at your local home improvement store. These magazines showcase the latest trends in design and products as well as offer helpful tips and advice.

You can also visit your local library to look for design magazines or even remodeling books. Remember, you can choose your kitchen cabinets from one magazine, the countertop pattern you like from the internet, then a backsplash plan from a local do it yourself store. Combining what you like from all of these different sources is what makes the kitchen unique and not a carbon copy of someone else's plan.

Model Homes

Visiting model homes is another great way to see the latest and greatest out there in kitchen design, materials and colors. These models are designed and decorated by professionals to get your attention. Their goal is to make you want to live there so why not use their expertise to help you plan your own amazing kitchen.

To avoid the sales pitch and hassle be up front with the real estate agents at the model home. Tell them you are looking at remodel ideas, not planning on purchasing a new house. As long as you are respectful of their potential clients, they will let you look as long as you like. You can even snap a few pictures of things you like to take with you.

One of the best things about model homes is you can see the actual materials performing in person. This means that the floors are being walked on, the counters and cabinets are being touched. You will notice some of these materials show dirt, dust and handprints more readily than others.

This is something to take into account when you plan your own materials. If you have a very busy kitchen, especially one that will have lots of little hands helping you, you might not want a material that shows every handprint. Some stainless steel appliance and high gloss cabinet finishes are very beautiful but require a lot of maintenance to keep all of the smudges, handprints and water marks off them on a daily basis. They may not be the best choice for a busy family kitchen.

Other materials will be more forgiving, you won't have to clean them every day. Overall, lighter materials seem to show less dirt and handprints than darker or shinier materials, however, using the darker materials can make the most dramatic looks too so take some time and choose your materials carefully.

Besides looking for material you like, look at the color combinations you are drawn to as well. Also, decide what you don't like so you can eliminate those options right away. It is so much easier to judge the colors on a big, room-sized scale than looking at the small samples you will see in the design center of the contractor or local showroom. Often the real estate agents have display boards in their office that will give you the manufacturer's name and color. You can take this information to your contractor to match with similar products he offers so don't be afraid to ask to see the boards.

Model homes are also a great way to get inspiration for your kitchen backsplash or accent paint. A backsplash area has a lot of options from flamboyant colors or dramatic patterns to simple and elegant designs, depending on your taste and design choice. Model homes often have a combination of these using tile, paint and even countertop material to create unique looks. Check them out and make notes or take pictures of the things you like to show your designer or contractor.

Another way to use model home kitchens when planning your kitchen is you can find them in a huge price range. What I mean is, there are lower priced homes and higher priced homes. This means that the kitchen materials used in the homes will be lower or higher priced as well, depending on the home price. So, you will see the best of the best in your price range no matter which range you are looking.

One comment on visiting model homes is to be careful not to fall in love with the half a million dollar home kitchen when your home budget would realistically fall closer to $20,000 - $50,000. Stick to looking at things that are practical for your home and your budget. Look at model homes priced closer to what you would spend on a new house, which will help you stay within a reasonable budget for the home you are remodeling.

After all, you will never see a good return on investment if you overbuild your home for its current area. This means that if your house and the houses in the surrounding area are valued at $200,000, your home won't automatically be valued at $275,000 if you put in a $75,000 kitchen remodel. Be reasonable about what materials to choose and dollar amount to invest in your home.

The best return on investment for a kitchen remodel is to plan to spend between 6% and 10% of the home's value. This price range will give you the correct materials and features suited to your home in a resale market. If you are not sure about your home's current value and how much you should reasonably invest in a remodel, talk to a local real estate agent. They will offer some free advice in the hopes that you will remember their helpfulness and will pass their name along or you will use them yourself if you find you are in need of an agent.

So, by visiting a few model homes you get a quick peek into what is new and trending in your area. You can get an idea the types of materials you should plan for in the price range of your current home too. After you check out the kitchens in these model homes, you will be in a better position to make an informed decision about what you want your kitchen to look like.

Home Shows

Home shows are a great place to find inspiration for your new kitchen. Home shows are a gathering of vendors who have remodeling services, home décor or other home improvement items to offer.

Home shows will have at least a few full kitchen set ups to look at. There will also be a lot of material samples like kitchen cabinet door options and flooring choices. In addition, most kitchen remodeling contractors, cabinet companies and countertop companies will have sample products and photographs to look at as well. Some may have a nice before / after book with examples of the transformations they have been involved in. These before and after pictures can be very helpful because you will probably find some before photographs that look very like your own current kitchen. Then, when you look at the after pictures, you can truly get a vision of how different and amazing your space can become.

The real beauty about home shows is that you can actually get a lot of your work done here. You will have contractors and designers and everything you need under one roof. You can speak to multiple designers and contractors on the same day to help you pick the perfect match to remodel your home. As there is a highly competitive environment at home shows, they often offer special deals and you can bet you will get the best value for your money.

However, don't allow yourself to be rushed into making an on the spot decision or signing a contract that same day. An honest contractor with nothing to hide will still honor that show special if you take a few days to decide. Just talk to them both at the show about your remodel and make sure you follow up with them at the office (or by phone or email) no more than a few days later.

Use this time to look the company up with the local better business bureau, Angie's list or other places clients can give feedback and reviews. After all, you want the best you can get and don't need to settle for someone with a questionable reputation. Remember, you get what you pay for and sometimes a bargain isn't always a good deal.

Home shows in your area are usually easy to find. Look at the "Things to Do" in the local newspaper, watch for billboards, television or radio advertisements. Usually they are held in local convention centers or other large venues. Sometimes there is a nominal charge to enter but having everyone under one roof so you can do some planning and information gathering is well worth the price of the ticket.

Create a Checklist

By now you have a collection of design ideas for your kitchen. Although you would love to use all these ideas to build the ultimate kitchen you need to be mindful of the fact that you will have a budget to adhere to. This means you will need to prioritize and shortlist these ideas until you establish the biggest priorities for the new kitchen. It is important that you include must have items first, then you can include a separate wish list if there is money left over in your budget.

The best way to do this is to create a checklist of what is important to you. Keep in mind what you really want and need. For example, if granite countertops are very important to you, you may need to look at less expensive woods for your cabinet doors than you originally planned. Staying within budget will be a balancing act, but one that you can win if you keep good records to track your budget and expenses. The worksheets provided at the end of the book will help you do this very well.

Another great way to stay on budget is to have a secondary plan or choice for some items. This way, if you have to bump up your spending in one area, you are prepared for where the money will come from by decreasing your spending in another. If you decide to put in those extra fancy door pulls, you might need to find some less expensive lighting to keep your funding balanced.

If you are hoping to change your kitchen layout, create rough drawings that you can share with designers who will use their expertise to convert them into detailed drawings for contractors to follow. Remember, changing plumbing, walls, cabinet or appliance locations can greatly increase the cost of your project so make sure you get several bids before make your final decision to do this.

If you have pictures of things that you like, gather them in one place to show your contractor and/or designer because this will help them share your vision for the new kitchen.

As you decide what look and functionality you are going for it becomes easier to choose your actual materials.

Here is an example of a kitchen remodel checklist of priorities:

Our Dream Kitchen
1. Modern looking cabinets with more drawers/slide outs
2. Granite or quartz countertops
3. Enlarge island to provide seating for guests
4. New flooring-wood look (can tear out / lay new ourselves if necessary to stay in budget)
5. Under cabinet lighting (can install ourselves)
6. Barstools for island (can purchase later)
7. New dining table and chairs to match kitchen (can purchase later)
8. Large single bowl undermount sink
9. Matching granite or quartz backsplash (if in budget)
10. Matching cabinet/stone vanity in guest bathroom

Chapter 3: Budgeting and Financing Your Kitchen Project

Of course, the next step in designing your new kitchen is setting your budget. The first thing to decide is how much you have to spend. How do you plan to finance your project? For some people this can be as simple as breaking open that piggy bank to see how much you have saved. If you do not have savings set aside to cover this remodel, what is your plan?

Sometimes a refinance or home equity loan is the way to go if your home has appreciated. Remember, a remodeled kitchen can increase both the resale appeal and the value of your home so don't automatically discount borrowing against your home to get the kitchen of your dreams.

However, make sure that the repayment plan is reasonable for you and your family to take on at this time in your life, even if the remodel is part of a bigger plan to make the home more marketable when you put it up for sale. Talk to your accountant or banker to see if a secured loan or other financing is good option for you. Do this before you start talking with contractors so you have some idea of a budget before you start.

Also, loans will take some time to process, especially if you are refinancing your home with a cash out option to pay for the remodel. Make sure you and your contractor know the payment options and dates so that you can be sure funding is available to make these payments.

Generally, in any contracting work there will be deposits made up front before the work begins. This money is to cover the cost of the materials they are ordering for your kitchen (cabinets, countertop materials, etc.) The payment schedules will vary from contractor to contractor so don't assume your contractor will have the same payment expectations as another. It is best to get the payment schedule in writing before you sign the contract.

With either a cash or loan plan, it will be important that you set your budget and stick to it. The best plan is to set a budget about 10 to 20% less than you have to spend on the project, this way you have a cushion if there are any overruns or unexpected surprises. It really sucks to have to find additional money you didn't plan for if there is an unexpected problem during demolition! After all, by this time your cabinets and other materials have already been ordered and received so changing these for less expensive items are no longer a project option.

So how do you set a budget for your kitchen remodel? It is easy to know what you want, however, the aim is to know how much you can afford. We need to set a realistic budget. Not one that is so small it leads to a cheap remodeling job; neither should we set a limit which is too extravagant. Remember, if we end up spending too much on the remodeling job we might not get enough returns to justify it if we sell the home. A general rule of thumb in the industry suggests spending about 15% of the home's value on a kitchen remodel. But this is just a guideline, you can spend less, or more but don't expect to recoup all of the money if you upgrade too much for your home's area and size.

To get an idea where you money will go here is the National Kitchen & Bath Association average breakdown on kitchen remodel costs:

> 29% on cabinetry & hardware
> 17% on labor (installation/demolition)
> 14% on appliances and ventilation
> 10% on countertops
> 7% on flooring
> 5% on lighting
> 4% on faucets & plumbing
> 4% on design fees

10% on other miscellaneous (windows/doors/walls, etc.)

Cabinets

As you can see from the information previous, your cabinets are usually the biggest expense in a kitchen remodel. There is a huge range of prices for kitchen cabinets. They can cost as little as $75 per linear foot to over $1,000 per linear foot. This means that cabinets for the same L shaped kitchen can range from $2,250 to $30,000 just for the cabinets. That is a huge difference in price and quality here. There are three main classes of cabinets set by the industry, economy, premium and custom. However, even within these broad terms there are so many ranges that it is best to talk with your contractor and closely examine the cabinets he proposes to use. Keep in mind that "all wood" is not the same as "solid wood" because particleboard and pressed board can be called "all wood" since they are still made of wood. Better quality cabinets are solid wood.

Now is the time to be honest with yourself...what do you really need in a kitchen cabinet? Are solid wood, unique or customized cabinets really important to you? Do you need them taller (or shorter) than the standard 36 inch height? Does your kitchen have an unusual layout, like angled walls or odd corners? If you answered yes to any of these then you may need to look at totally custom built cabinet options to get what you need.

Then again, maybe you want a great looking, custom kitchen but don't have any special cabinet size needs. A semicustom cabinet option is probably just what you need. A semicustom cabinet starts with premade boxes and are adjusted to suit client needs. They are typically the standard height, but some adjustments can be made. The cabinets are faced with solid wood and have solid wood doors. This is an excellent compromise that will get you a fabulous, durable look for a good middle of the road price.

Be aware that you can cut corners on your cabinets and go with the laminate doors too but be careful you don't cut corners too much. Inexpensive, poorly made cabinets will not hold up well in a busy kitchen. Remember that saying, you get what you pay for? This can be very true when selecting your new kitchen cabinets.

Shop around and examine workmanship carefully. Laminate is okay if they are well made and the wood used for the laminate is of a good quality. No matter how good those economy cabinets look in the glossy magazine, look at a sample of the actual cabinet grade your contractor will be putting in your kitchen. This way there are no surprises in quality when all those boxes arrive at the door.

Refacing your existing cabinets could be an option for you if you want to save a little money. Consider this option only if your existing cabinets are in great shape, are real wood and you don't want to make any design changes to the layout. Refacing will be about 20 to maybe 30% cheaper than buying all new cabinets.

Something to consider when thinking about refacing is it isn't going to save you a ton of money over new cabinets. This is simply because the fronts, doors and accessories are often the most expensive part of the cabinet. Your kitchen reface will probably take a little less time to complete than new cabinets. However, you will still need to remove the contents since they have to remove all of the doors to take to their shop, reskin all of the visible cabinet sides, then replace the doors and install new hardware. You won't want your dishes in there while they are working because they will be in the way and they will end up dusty and dirty.

Also, installing new cabinets instead of refacing will allow you to take advantage of all of the new slide outs, racks and other features not traditionally built into older cabinets. Sure, some of these features can be added to your older cabinets for a price, but now you have easily worked your budget up to the same price as getting all new, modern cabinets in the first place.

Countertops

Some kitchen remodeling projects allow you to keep your original cabinets, just reface them with new wood skins or paint them to change the color. Usually there are not too many options that allow you to save your existing countertops so plan on replacing them. The exception is if you already have an expensive material. If you are hoping to save your countertops, it will be even more critical that you find a really qualified installer because it is difficult to remove installed countertops, especially granite, without damaging it.

Countertop prices can vary a great deal depending on the material you choose. Usually the most budget friendly option will be to use laminate materials. High end granite materials are at the top of the budget and there is a huge range in between.

The current trends in kitchen countertops use a lot of granite and quartz products which are extremely strong and durable. Even on a budget, there are ways to find reasonable prices for some of these products, so talk to your local contractors to see what kind of deals they may have.

Flooring

If you are considering updating your flooring in the kitchen area, now is the time to get the quotes. It is much easier to tear out and install new flooring now than six months after you have had new cabinets installed. You may save money contracting the floor replacement from a separate installer.

Then again, it is sometimes worth a little extra money to have one contractor coordinating the efforts of all of the workers. Get several quotes before you decide what will work best for you.

There are a huge range of flooring choices for your kitchen in a wide range of prices. You can choose from laminate to tile, wood to painted concrete and each of these has many different looks and styles. Materials like carpet are not recommended for installation in the kitchen because of the difficulty in keeping them clean. Unsealed natural stone is also not always the best choice in the kitchen as it can become stained easily by products like olive oil, red wine or other foods.

Along the same note, think about the type of use your kitchen gets. Smaller grout lines and smoother tile surfaces will make the material easier to clean. However, tile that has a very high gloss finish may become slick when wet, which can be a hazard in the kitchen where water and other liquids do end up on the floor. Lighter colors will show less dust and dirt than dark surfaces, but dark surfaces can hide spills and stains easier.

Choose your flooring material first, then select a pattern and colors that compliment or accent your cabinet and countertop choices. If you are lucky and shop around, you can often find some great flooring materials on sale or at a discount. Whichever material you choose, you will have a variety of color and pattern options to complete the look you are going for in your new kitchen.

Chapter 4: Designing Your New Space

We reach the most exciting phase of our kitchen/bath remodeling project. We have laid the groundwork by doing all our homework.

Up until this point we have decided what we want, budgeted and arranged finance, hired a designer and picked a contractor.

Things are finally set in motion now as we finalize all our choices. This is the time the trio gets together which is the home owner, designer and contractor.

Everything is discussed and finalized before actual work begins.

There is so much to do and remember that it can be overwhelming at times. Which is why we are here to simplify everything for you. Based on our experience working on kitchen/bath remodeling projects we know what needs to be done and the order in which it needs to be done.

We will break up each task that goes into designing your new kitchen/bath space to ensure nothing is left out. By the time we are done with this chapter your contractor will be ready and raring to go ahead with the remodeling.

Choose a Layout

The design for your kitchen begins by choosing a layout. A layout is a floor plan which will decide where cabinets, appliances and fixtures are. There are a number of different layouts to choose from. Maybe you already have a layout you like that works for you. Nevertheless there is no harm in considering new layouts. Who knows you might just like one.

It is crucial to get your heart set on a layout of your choice. Listen to what the designer and contractor has to say as they are experienced and will know how to make optimum use of space available. Your designer might even create a custom layout for your kitchen.

Each layout is different and what worked in your friend's kitchen might not be the right layout for yours. The key is to ensure that an area like the kitchen which has a lot of footfall is comfortable and easy to use for everybody in the family.

Here are a few tried and tested layouts you will find in kitchens around the world.

L Shaped Kitchen Layout

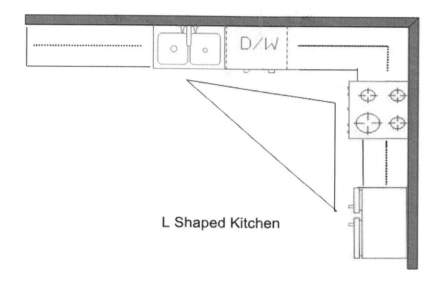

L Shaped Kitchen

The L shaped kitchen layout is one of the most popular modern kitchen layouts. Based on decades of research in ergonomics it is the most efficient kitchen layout by far. An L shaped kitchen layout involves arranging the three 'legs' which is the refrigerator, cook top and sink in an L shape. The workspace is arranged against two walls which are perpendicular to each other creating a right angled triangle. This adheres to the fundamentals of work triangle which we will discuss later.

L shaped kitchen layouts can also have an island at the center which could be a seating area so that it is easy to serve to family members and guests. It leads to a good conversation space as you can talk while you are cooking. An L shaped kitchen also means you can have a co-chef in the kitchen working simultaneously without getting in the way of each other.

L shaped kitchen areas require more space if you choose to include the island sitting area. However if you decide to skip the island you can make an L Shaped layout work for your kitchen.

An L shaped kitchen layout's length can be adjusted according to the space available and are great for corner space.

U (or C) Shaped Kitchen Layout

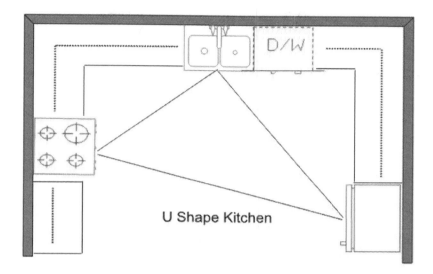

U Shape Kitchen

U Shaped kitchen layout is all about high efficiency cooking and can maximize cabinet and counter space. The layout of the kitchen forms a "U" shape with the cabinets, walls and countertops forming the lines of the U. The open top of the U is the entry into and out of this space.

Some U shaped kitchens are large spaces but this probably the most efficient use of small kitchen spaces. It will allow you to maximize the cabinet and countertop space in a limited area.

The cook can easily move from cooktop to the sink or refrigerator as most U shaped kitchens do not include a center island. Usually you will want to place the refrigerator at the outer edge of the U near the entrance to the kitchen. You do this so that other members of the family can access the refrigerator without getting in the way of the person working in the kitchen.

The advantage of this layout is that you can add lots of cabinet and counter space because you work across 3 sides, not two as in an L shaped kitchen. Some U shaped kitchens will have one section open, no wall behind the countertop, to create a convenient eating bar along one side of the space. The people seated are on the outside of the kitchen facing in, so it is easy to converse with them without having them under foot while you are working in the kitchen.

G Shaped Kitchen Layout

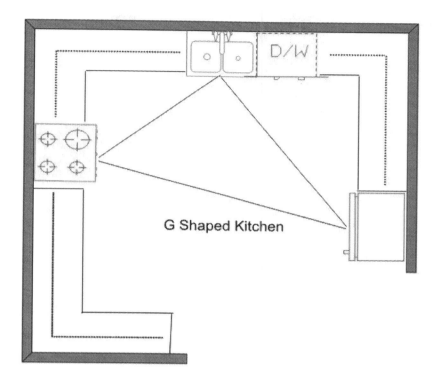

G Shaped Kitchen

The G shaped kitchen layout uses the same principles as the U (or C) shaped kitchen. The only difference here is a wall, or often a seating area, comes out along one of the walls into the open part of the U. This means a smaller entry area into the kitchen but added cabinets, counter or seating space.

Island or Peninsula shaped kitchen layout

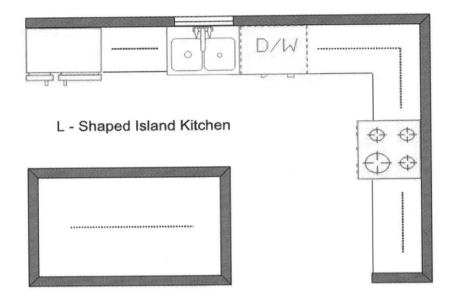

L - Shaped Island Kitchen

Sounds tropical however the island kitchen layout is the most popular layout with home owners with large kitchen area. It makes use of all the space that is available and has potential to add large number of cabinets and kitchen counters. It is a style of kitchen you associate with big spacious homes. There is enough space for two to cook together and guests can move in and out without getting in the way.

A peninsula shaped layout is made up of two or more work spaces with one against the wall while other is free standing and perpendicular. It is an easy way to divide the kitchen workspace in to different zones. Cabinets, counters and appliances however may not be within reach and require the cook to move back and forth.

Island or peninsula styled kitchen layouts are best for open floor space and is adjustable to any length or width.

Galley or corridor kitchen layout

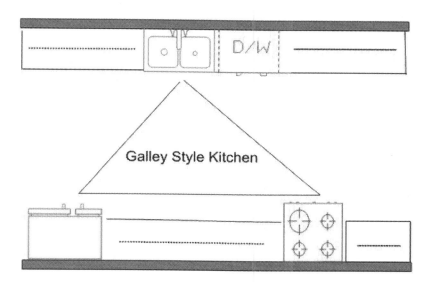

Galley Style Kitchen

The galley or corridor kitchen layout also makes the best use of smaller space; it is all about maximizing what is available. It was one of the most popular styles in the 80's and you can still find kitchens using this layout. The layout is called galley because it closely resembles the galley on planes and ships. It is the best option for homes where space is a premium. A galley kitchen is open at both ends, with the kitchen cabinets, appliances and countertops placed parallel to each other in the space.

Galleys usually place the refrigerator and food storage area near the open ends of the kitchen. This is done so that family members do not get in the way of each other while making trips to the refrigerator.

The galley layout works well when you have just one wall usable for kitchen space or when your space is long and narrow. Sometimes in a galley kitchen, the dining table is at the far side of the kitchen. This layout, or one with a partially open area on one side of the kitchen with bar stools makes the galley style kitchen easier to entertain in than the often one person work space that fully enclosed galley kitchens can be.

Choose the best use of your available space using the principals of these standard layouts. Another advantage of hiring a designer is that they can plan and help you visualize which of these will work best for your space. They can even create a custom layout for your kitchen if required.

Setting up the Work Triangle

There is one fundamental principle which should be followed regardless of which kitchen layout you choose. It is known as the work triangle and is based upon decades of ergonomic studies and real world experiences.

The principle is founded on the understanding that the cooktop, refrigerator and sink are the three main points in a kitchen. A kitchen cannot do without any one of these and thus they are referred to as the legs.

When you draw imaginary lines between the cooktop, refrigerator and sink you get a work triangle. The idea is that these three elements need to be near each other but not in close proximity for the kitchen to run efficiently. The rule of thumb for a work triangle is that the space between each leg should not be less than four feet or more than 9 feet. Also, there should be no exterior traffic flow within the triangle to ensure nobody gets in the way of the person cooking.

When setting up the kitchen layout you should also make sure there are no tall cabinets inside this area because they will interfere with the workflow. Each area of the triangle, should have at least 2 feet of counter space available next to them to allow you to set objects and work around the appliances efficiently.

So no matter which layout you choose do ensure it creates an efficient work triangle.

Choosing Materials and Styles

You will need to decide on the materials that will be used for countertops and cabinets. Your designer and contractor will provide a list of materials from which you can choose. However for your convenience we have listed a few of them below. Prices for these products can vary a great deal depending on the current availability of products and your area so we did not include prices for these products.

Granite- Granite is the most popular countertop choice today and we can see why. It truly brings the variety and beauty of nature indoors. It is tough and can withstand rough usage. This is natural stone does need to be sealed occasionally to prevent staining from items such as red wine or olive oil, however, the newest techniques now seal so well that products are often warrantied for up to 10 years or more against staining.

Granite or any stone countertop material is heavier than solid surface, laminate and tile which makes installation best done by professionals. Most cabinets on the market, except possibly the very low end economy grades, are strong enough to support granite as the weight is distributed across a large area very evenly. If you live in a much older home, your contractor should examine the floor and under the floor to determine if any additional joists or support are needed under the cabinets before adding the weight of granite or any stone countertop material to your kitchen.

Another disadvantage to granite is that although a really strong and durable product, it cannot be repaired if something happens to it like solid surface or other manmade products can be. It is very important that cabinets be level to prevent cracking of the stone from its own weight. Granite is very heat and scratch resistant so hot pans and cookware will not mar the surface.

The cost of granite countertops will vary a great deal depending on a few factors. The first one is the granite you choose. Some granites are very reasonably priced because they are in good supply and are easy to work with. Other granite slabs can be 10 times or more the price of other slabs because of the scarcity of the stone. Some of the most expensive stone is also the toughest to work with and you could end up buying more than you planned on if there are problems in manufacturing.

To keep costs down, ask to see the stone slabs in the lower price ranges first to see if there are any you like. These lower priced granites are not lesser quality, in fact often these are stronger than the fancier exotic stone. The patterns may not be as dramatic or unique in their patterning, but then again they will usually be more uniform and give you a better resale as the more neutral or evenly distributed patterns will appeal to a wider range of people when you do sell your home.

Quartz Composites – This material is becoming more and more popular because it is as tough as it is beautiful. Stronger than most other stone products it also extremely scratch and heat resistant. Many people also like the fact the colors and patterns are so consistent throughout the material.

Marble – Marble has a very lavish feel to it and is popular material in kitchen these days. Nothing beats marble when it comes to elegance and it is tough too. It can stand up to heat well however since it is softer than granite and other stone solutions, it is prone to both scratching and staining.

Manufactured Stone (Silestone, etc) -Manufactured stone has many of the same properties as real granite or quartz. It is available under several different brand names so talk to your contractor about the stone products available in your area.

The nice part about manufactured stone is it is impervious to heat and does not scratch easily (you will never scratch it with a knife or other kitchen tools). This stone is also completely nonporous and you will not need to seal or coat it like you will natural stone products.

Manufactured stone does come in a variety of colors and the patterns, unlike many natural stone products, are very consistent from slab to slab as well as throughout the slab. This product is about as expensive as natural stone but is very low maintenance, extremely durable and is a great choice in a heavy use kitchen.

Solid Surface (Corian and other similar materials) – Solid surface materials like Corian are an easy care solution to your countertop needs. The beauty of this material is that there are hundreds of color choices, colors are consistent throughout the pattern and seems are virtually invisible when installed by an experienced crew.

You can have built in drain boards and sinks of the same material too. Edge details are limitless and can even have inlays of different colors in not only the edges but virtually anywhere on the countertop as the material can be glued together with virtually no visible seam on most colors.

Although the product is not resistant to heat and can crack if a pan straight from the oven is placed on the surface. Since it is manmade, it is possible to repair cracks, burns or other damage to the countertops without having to replace the whole countertop, which you would have to do with granite or quartz. Also, because it is manmade it is easier to color match if you want to add material later or need to repair damage.

Scratches and shallow cuts in the surface of the material can be sanded out and solid surface is easy to clean. Since the material is nonporous it will not harbor bacteria like wood can.

Concrete – Concrete comes and goes as a popular material to use in kitchen countertops. Concrete is easy to mix on site and can even have stains applied to make it a variety of colors. Many home owners also choose to add inlays such as glass fragments, tiles, wood, sea shells and stones to bring color and texture into their concrete countertops.

Concrete, as you know, is tough and can withstand rough usage. Concrete countertops do need to be properly installed over very level cabinets to avoid cracking. Concrete can be fixed but not easily and it is a very porous material, so you will need to seal it regularly to avoid staining by products such as red wine and olive oil.

Stainless steel – Stainless steel is used on large scale in commercial kitchens. It is durable and yet lighter than concrete or quartz. It is also versatile and can be molded into any shape you need, sometimes without seams.

This material is completely nonporous, does not stain but can be scratched or dented. Also, although stainless steel is nearly indestructible it is a fingerprint magnet and needs to be wiped down frequently with special stainless steel cleaners to keep it looking good. If you like the industrial look then stainless steel is the material for you.

Wood – Wood on countertops and islands is making a comeback these days. The wood is treated with fire retardant solution and can withstand heat.
It is also sturdy as well as light in weight. The downsides to wood are it needs oiling and sealing frequently to avoid staining. It is also porous and can harbor bacteria if not cared for properly.

The upside to wood is that it can be sanded to remove scratches and stains that do no soak too far into the wood.

Tile - Tile is a very versatile product and comes in an endless range of colors, patterns, textures and even natural granite and quartz. This is a great way to create a completely customized look for your kitchen that extends not only your countertops, but a coordinating backsplash too.

Tile can be significantly less expensive than some of the other countertop materials out there, quartz or solid surface, and unlike most stone slabs or solid surface materials can even be installed by you if you are up to the challenge.

The downside to tile countertops comes in the grout lines as they can be problematic to keep clean and can make your work surface uneven. The large the tile chosen, the fewer the grout lines you will have. In addition, some products, like quartz, can have very thin grout lines between them so these lines can be less noticeable and easier to keep clean than the wider ones necessary with most ceramic tiles.

Grout lines will need to be sealed regularly to keep them from staining and harboring bacteria so there is more maintenance from year to year than a manufactured stone, quartz or laminate kitchen. However, if tile becomes chipped, cracked or damaged, you can remove the damaged tile and replace them with new tile. To make this possible, order a few more tiles than you need and store them in case you need to make repairs years down the line.

Paper Composite- Yes that is right paper is used these days as material in the kitchen. This sustainable product is called Paperstone, however this is not like paper origami, as the name suggests. It is paper mixed with other materials such as resin that forms a composite which is both durable as well as eco-friendly.

If you thought it could be a fire hazard in the kitchen then think again. Paper composite is fire retardant and can even withstand water. Being lighter than any other material makes it a good option to be used in kitchen. Although starting to become more popular because of their low carbon footprint and eco-friendly market, paper composite countertops are still quite as expensive.

Laminate – Since the 1950's laminate countertops have been a popular choice in many kitchens. Laminate will cost a small fraction of what most other materials will and they come in literally hundreds of colors and patterns.

Although laminates can be damaged by heat and cut by knives, they are nonporous and easy to maintain bacteria free. With the new colors and pattern, they can even look like granite or even wood if you like.

A seamless backsplash can be built into your countertop and there are a variety of edge details available to give you different looks. There are even some laminate countertops that you can use with under mount sinks for a look similar to those found in more expensive granite kitchens.

If you are looking for an easy maintenance kitchen on a budget, check out the many varieties and patterns on laminate available for today's modern kitchens. With all the choices available there is sure to be something in the look you want. After all, because didn't spend a fortune on the material, you can even afford to change it out after a few years to a new color or pattern to give your kitchen a completely new look.

Sinks

Kitchen sinks come in a huge variety of sizes, shapes, colors and materials. Take some time to think about how you use your sink before you choose a new one. Choosing your new sink should be first about function, then second choose a style that coordinates with the look you are looking for.

Some sinks have two equal sections, allowing you to do two things at once at the sink. These are called 50/50 sinks. For example, you can wash your dishes on one side and rinse them on the other. Or maybe you need to have a place to wash your fruit and a place to wash your hands on the other.

Other sinks have two bowls but one is much larger than the other, maybe a 60/40 split or even a 70/30 split. Here you have one small bowl to so things like rinse items or wash your hands, then a larger bowl to wash pans or other large items.

Another style used in kitchens is to have one large sink with no dividers. These sinks are great if you wash many large items like big saucepans, crockpots or roasting pans. They do have their drawbacks though because you will not have a second bowl to utilize while something is soaking in the single bowl.

The last sink used in kitchens is the farmhouse style sink, which is becoming popular in many new country style kitchens. This sink does require special installation and a modified cabinet to put it in since it rests right to the front, with no countertop or cabinet front between the sink and you. These sinks will be more costly both to purchase and install so they are not a good choice for the tight budget.

When choosing a sink, look at how that model is to be mounted. How you can mount the sink will vary with the countertop material you are using and the style of sink you are choosing. Don't be afraid to ask questions or see a diagram if you aren't sure what the mount and the sealing lines will look like. Some sinks drop in a hole cut into the countertop. These models have a lip around the top that rests the sink on top of the counter. This edge will be caulked to prevent water from seeping under it.

Other sinks are undermounted. This means they are attached to the countertop from below. They can be undermounted several different ways. One way is with the top edge of the sink visible. In this mount style there will be a countertop, a drop to the top of the sink, then a small rim around the sink. Sometimes this can be difficult to keep clean. Another way to undermount is flush with the countertop so there is only a small sealer line along where the sink and the countertop material comes together. The last is to mount the sink so that the countertop opening is slightly smaller than the sink opening. In this style you will not see the caulk lines and there are no ridges to collect water and food particles.

Don't just look at pictures of sinks because it is hard to get a feel for how large, deep or shallow they really are from a picture. Go out and look at some different sinks, either at a warehouse showroom like Home Depot, or in a design showroom at a home show or remodeling supply store. Your contractor may have several different style in his warehouse/fabrication facility that you can look at as well. It is always best to see the sink before you have it installed because once it is mounted it cannot be easily changed, especially in granite or other natural stone.

There are several different common kitchen sink materials to choose from as well. Most common is the stainless steel sink. These are great because they are inexpensive and very durable. The stainless steel is very resistant to damage if you buy the higher grade steel. The lower the number, the higher the grade of steel. The most common grades to use for kitchen sinks are between 18 and 22 gauge steel. The higher number sinks can dent and may be noisier than the lower numbers if you drop items into them but they are still resistant to stains and heat.

Next in popularity are the granite or quartz composite sinks. These are very popular with homeowners installing granite or quartz countertops. They are made of ground up stone mixed with a strong resin filler. This material is forced into a form to make the sinks. Granite sinks come in a variety of colors to coordinate with the stone products and are extremely heat and scratch resistant. They are heavier than stainless steel and sometimes additional bracing must be done underneath to support them. They can also come with a higher price tag than stainless steel sinks.

If you are installing solid surface materials like Corian you can also get a sink of the same material as well. These sinks have smooth, seamless mounting when used with solid surface countertops and come in several coordinating colors. Their pricing is very reasonable and they have the same strong, nonporous properties as the countertops. If you are using this material for your countertops, consider investing in the coordinating sinks as well. You will love the seamless look and feel.

Cast iron is another way to go when looking at material for your sink. Some antique cast iron sinks are still in demand today because of the durability and beauty. The enamel coatings used today are even stronger than some of those antique items. Because they are iron underneath the porcelain enamel glaze these sinks can be extremely heavy so installation can be difficult and require additional supports underneath. The sinks do come in a variety of sizes, shapes and even colors to match your kitchen. Be aware that these colors do come at a premium and can boost the cost of the sink hundreds of dollars. The enamel on cast iron sinks is very strong but if it does become damaged there are some ways to repair them.

Fireclay is used to make the farmhouse style sinks, among other styles. These sinks are sometimes considerably more expensive than other models listed. Fireclay sinks typically come in white but some can be found in other colors, typically black or shades of brown. They are durable and fashionable but they do come with a price tag to match.

Faucets

Buying a good quality faucet when you remodel your kitchen is important. The faucet in most kitchens is a heavy use item...you use it to wash dishes, cook your food, wash your hands....literally everything you do in the kitchen uses the faucet and sink. Budget a little more and buy for quality.

Some of the best features for kitchen sinks are faucets that will pull out to allow you to direct the water in the direction you need it. These faucets also often have a button to change the spray pattern from a stream to more of a shower, which comes in very handy when rinsing things like fruits and vegetables.

Since most countertops need holes drilled to accommodate the faucet layout, you will need to purchase and have the faucet on site when the countertop and sink are installed. Since holes are being placed into the countertop, it won't be that easy to switch to a completely different faucet style if you decide you don't like yours down the road. So if you think you really want two handles, one for cold and one for hot, get it now instead of the single handle faucet. Otherwise you will have the wrong hole pattern drilled.

Faucets also add a lot of unique style to your kitchen and can help complete the look you are after. They are almost an accessory or decorator touch on top of being functional and durable. As you choose a faucet, think about cleaning, maintaining and using the faucet. You might not want those very elaborate faucet handles if you think it will be difficult to keep them clean. And although a waterfall faucet is very unique and beautiful can you use it to wash the dishes in your sink?

Some of the newest features in sinks are the touchless kitchen faucets. These faucets have sensors in them that you trigger to turn them on. They will stay on a set time then turn off. You have probably used them in restrooms before. They might seem like a great idea because you don't have to touch handles or anything to wash your dirty hands in the kitchen.

However, think about all the times you are doing things at the sink when you don't want the water to go on. This can be annoying since you will inadvertently pass the sensor sometimes no matter how careful you try to be. Also, they don't have the same flow control that you get with a standard faucet. Sometimes you need a hard flow to fill that large pan but sometimes a soft flow is what you need when rinsing those delicate sprouts. Think twice before investing in this very expensive kitchen gadget. If you use your kitchen a lot you will probably find yourself replacing it for a traditional faucet that you can control.

A built in soap dispenser is another great tool many people are adding to the sink area of their new kitchens. Just choose a pump style that coordinates with your faucet and your contractor will install it when he drills the holes for the sink. The soap holder is underneath and you fill it by lifting the dispenser or unscrewing the soap container from below. This can eliminate the need for messy soap bottles on the back of the sink.

Lighting Options

Great lighting will bring out the beauty of your new kitchen. It is also important to have good lighting when working in the kitchen. The best lighting in your kitchen will be a good mix of natural, recessed, ceiling mounted and under cabinet lighting. The accessories you choose to provide the lighting will also tie the whole project together and add those custom touches that guests will really notice.

As we mentioned before what color you used for your kitchen also plays a role in choosing the lighting options. For instance the color white bounces light and reflects it on surface around it. If you paint your kitchen walls white and have white or light colored cabinets you will probably use lower wattage bulbs or less lights than if you have dark wood cabinets or darker accent walls.

To light the kitchen with a soft light, recessed lighting placed all around the area is a great start. Then, add some accent lighting to showcase and accent your style.

Spotlights are another great way to provide the light you need in the kitchen. Focus the light over your most used work areas or locations in the kitchen you want to be noticed...like a special cabinet door or piece of artwork.

To focus light on an island or peninsula, use hanging lights above the work area. These hanging lights can be the perfect opportunity to show off your style as the globes that cover the bulbs some in an endless variety of colors, patterns and textures.

If you have chosen glass doors on any of your cabinets, you should consider installing lights inside these to bring out the beauty of the doors and the dishes you are showcasing inside these cabinets.

In conjunction with the other lights you should use under cabinet lighting to ensure there is enough light while preparing working at these countertops. A great option for under cabinet lighting in the kitchen is to use LEDs. These LEDs come on a strip that can be attached all along the bottom underside of the cabinet. If you install them on a dimmer switch you will be able to adjust the lights-bright for working, dimmer to accent the beauty of your countertops and backsplash.

The lights can be installed by you or you can ask the contractor about the costs of his staff doing it when they are there. Remember, if you need to do any wiring work inside the walls, this needs to be done before the backsplash is installed. If you are doing the lighting work yourself, you will need to be ready to finish your part in the evening between the different stages of construction. You won't always have a weekend to complete your part of the process unless you and your contractor plan ahead and schedule this time.

Chapter 5: Hiring a Designer

A dilemma faced by many homeowners looking to do a major remodel in their kitchen is if you should hire a designer to help you with planning the project. If you are not sure what you want your new kitchen to look like or are considering making changes to the existing layout, a designer is the way to go.

Designers will be up to date on the most recent trends, styles and products available for your kitchen. They can help you plan the most efficient use of your space and help you design a kitchen that is beautiful, functional and within your budget.

Before you make any payments to the designer ask to see their certifications and references. CKD stands for Certified Kitchen designers and Certified Master Kitchen and Bath designers (CMKBD). These are experts in the field and will have the experience you need to get the job done.

Designers should have a book with samples of their work in it for you to review as well. There are many out there claiming to be designers that haven't had any formal training. You don't want to spend your hard earned money or waste your time if they don't have much more experience than you designing kitchens.

Some designers are hired just to design your kitchen and will provide you with the mock ups to take to your contractor. Other designers will work as a general contractor handling management of the remodel from start to finish. These will usually have specific companies that they work with so you may not get to choose the companies so clarify these items up front with them.

Some remodeling contractors have designers on staff too and this can save you money and time. Ask to see their credentials and certifications too. Just make sure they are a real designer and not just a salesperson with design experience.

If you are making major changes to your kitchen that involve removing walls you may need to enlist the services of an architect to ensure the structural integrity of your home is maintain. These services will be considerably more expensive than a designer so shop around carefully. They charge up to $150 per hour and may also charge 10 to 15% of the project total. If you need one, ask your contractor for a recommendation of an architect he has worked with.

The Process of Hiring a Designer

Start your hiring process with a search for a designer who operates locally. You can begin your search by asking your friends and family who have done remodeling in their own homes for recommendations. If they were pleased with the job they will be happy to give you their referral.

Another way to search for kitchen designers is to look online. There are a number of websites like Houzz, Angie's list and NKBA where you can find information as well as just using a search engine like Bing. It is easy to find phone numbers and website addresses for designers. You can even look at their local reviews, if they have them.

If the designer has their own website you can easily browse pictures of work they have completed. You might also find feedback and testimonials on the website. Most websites won't have fees listed because they want you to call and talk to them. For complete peace of mind you can also check with the Better Business Bureau to see if there are any pending complaints or if their company and the companies they work with are in good standing.

As said before, these designers are often affiliated with or work directly with particular contractors and remodeling companies. Look at the reviews of not only the designer, but the companies they are affiliated with as well. Overall, trust your instincts too. If you like and feel comfortable with the designer when you meet them, it is probably a good choice. If you don't feel comfortable with them or feel like they are really listening to what you are saying, look elsewhere.

Associate Kitchen and Bath Designer - AKBD

Certified professional with a minimum of 2 years of kitchen and bath industry experience. – They must meet educational expectations and pass a test.

Certified Kitchen and Bath Professional - CKBP

Certified professional with a minimum of 5 years of experience in the kitchen and bath industry. This certification is more centered on project management, construction, product knowledge, materials and business expertise and not so much on design. This certification requires they meet minimum educational expectations and pass a test.

Certified Kitchen Designers - CKD

Have a minimum of 7 years of experience specifically on kitchen design. They know building codes and have extensive knowledge on materials, appliances and space planning. They are extremely experienced at creating concepts and drawing up plans that industry professionals will have no trouble understanding and implementing. They must also meet minimum educational expectations and pass an academic as well as a practical exam.

Certified Bathroom Designers - CBD

Exactly the same as CKD, only with bathroom design experience instead of kitchen design experience.

Certified Master Kitchen and Bath Designer - CMKBD

A designer with both the CKD and CBD certifications plus 10 years of additional experience in design after having achieved their first certification for at least 17 years of kitchen and bath design experience. They also must meet educational requirements and such.

For a more complete list of certifications and what it takes to achieve them you can visit the KNBA website at: www.nkba.org

Shortlist and Meet the Designer

Now that you have found a few designers, you can check out their portfolios online and shortlist the ones who you feel are the best pick for your project. Choose three of them to call and set an appointment to meet them and discuss the project.

The suggestion to talk to at least three is to give you a statistical sampling. You can use more than three but it isn't recommended to do less. Two is not really enough to get a good range of prices and services, but three gives you a pretty good comparison without taking too much extra time. At least two of the three you talk to should have similar prices and services.

When you make your initial phone call be sure to discuss their rates. All three of them should have comparable rates. If one is very different from the others, you can ask them why their rate is significantly higher or lower than others is the area. (You do not need to specify the names of the other designers if you don't feel comfortable revealing this.) Maybe they have some certification or extra experience that warrants the increased rate, but then again, maybe they don't. If you are not comfortable with their explanation, don't waste your time meeting them in person. Choose someone else instead.

Some of the designers may want to meet you at the remodel location to get a feel for the place, others will invite you to meet in their office first to make it convenient for them to show you items in their showroom or portfolio.

If you are meeting in their office, make sure you have your kitchen floor plan with you so they can get a feel for the scope of the project. Since this initial meeting is just to decide which designer you are using, don't expect to walk away with any specific kitchen design ideas.

Instead, focus on getting a feel for how the designer works. Ask to see their design portfolio. Do not be surprised if you don't like everything in their portfolio. After all, they were designing kitchens to fit the taste and style of their clients. A very diversified portfolio will probably represent a talented designer who really listens and follows the leads of their client.

However, if you find their all of their designs too modern or too old fashioned for your taste, they probably are not the designer for you. You should like at least some of the rooms in their portfolio.

Let the designer know about the budget allocated for your kitchen remodel. Designers can help you get the most bang for the buck, but some may try and get you to raise that budget a bit if they also have a vision for your kitchen. Be firm! Don't let them talk you into something you cannot afford. You are the one paying the bills, not them.

This meeting is the time to go over rates again and get an estimated cost for their services. When you select a designer, make sure you get the rates in writing and their contract estimate. You will also want to make sure you have a set payment schedule. They will probably ask for part of the money up front, with the balance paid upon your acceptance of the design. Acceptance of the design is not the same thing as completion of the work, so be ready to pay your designer before the work even begins.

When you have met with your top designer choices, make your selection carefully. The easiest way to do this, as with most choices, is to list the pros and cons of each. The most important factor in choosing your designer is to pick the one you feel the best connection too, the one you think is really listening to what you want and you can communicate with. Of course, price will always play a factor in these decisions too so make sure you are keeping it in your budget...you don't want to have to reduce your countertop budget to pay your designer!

Now that you have hired your designer it is time for the fun, planning your new kitchen. The designer will try to figure out what you want by asking you questions. You should in turn ask the designer questions about their prior projects and their ideas for your kitchen project.

Remember those pictures you gathered of kitchens you liked? Show these to your designer. Also give him or her copies of the lists you made, the one that talks about what you like and don't like about your current kitchen, and a prioritized list of what you want in the new kitchen. The more information you can give the designer, the easier it will be for them to get you just what you want.

Communication with the designer will be important. The better the communication between you, the easier it will be to design the kitchen of your dreams. It will be important for you to listen to their ideas too because they might have some great thoughts and advice that you may not have thought of.

The designer will let you know if a certain design idea you have is not feasible. However, drawing from their experience they will also provide alternative ideas. They will introduce you to design ideas you may have never thought of. Always remember you should not sacrifice function for beauty. What may look beautiful may not have a place in your kitchen remodel if it is not functional.

Chapter 6: The Hunt for a Great Contractor

Now that we have our dream kitchen designed, we need someone who will bring it to life. To accomplish this we want the best we can get. That is why the hunt for a great contractor is the most crucial phase of the whole process. The success or failure of the whole project depends on the quality of the company you bring in to make your vision a reality.

How to look for a contractor:

Like most things, sometimes the easiest way to find quality is to ask others who they recommend. Talk to your friends, family and coworkers to see who they have used for their kitchen. Most of us know at least a few people who have been through a kitchen remodel or know someone close to them who has.

If you have a designer, they will have recommendations for you as well. Some designers work very closely with local contractors. Take their recommendation list and go read the reviews that independent homeowners have written before you make a decision.

Next best way is to use the power of the internet. Sites like Angie's List and Houzz.com have lists of contractors in the area. What is great about these sites is that they have unbiased and verified feedback from lots of different people. You can also find contractors just doing a Google or Bing search in your area.

Attending a local home show to talk to contractors, look at products available and see before and after pictures will allow you to do a lot in one day. Bring your list of questions or just get contact information so that you can talk to them later when there is not so much going on around you and them.

Take your list of potential contractors and start your decision making process by looking up their record with the Better Business Bureau in your area. You can also get information on them from the Registrar of Contractors. You don't want to hire a contractor with lots of complaints from their customers or other businesses they work with.

Next, look online for reviews for the ones that are in good standing. If a contractor has one or two poor reviews but lots of positive reviews, you can feel comfortable keeping them on your list at least for now. Let's face it, we all know people that are sometimes impossible to please and very vocal about their displeasure too. Independent reviews are good, but you can also read testimonials the company has placed on its website. Yes, these testimonials will be only the positive feedback, but they do get them directly from their customers.

What to look for in contractor:

What you want is a contractor that has been in business for more than a couple of years. It would be best to have a contractor that has been in business at least 5 years and has a fantastic reputation. After all we are not looking for a good contractor, we want a great contractor, a rock star in the industry.

You want a contractor that has won awards. Although design awards are nice, what we are looking for are quality and customer service awards from major organizations, publications, or non-biased review sites.

You want a contractor that listens to you. If you find they are talking more than listening, you probably want to look elsewhere.

You want a contractor that isn't having a bunch of issues with the better business bureau or the association of contractors. It is easy to check by going to each organizations website or by giving them a call at their local phone number.

You want the contractor to be fully licensed and insured and willing and able to provide proof of both when requested.

You want a contractor that is happy to provide references to you. These should include a phone number where you can contact the person, but also the date when the work was completed. If all the references are more than a year old, ask for at least one more recent.

You want a contractor that will give you detailed bids for the job.

You want to avoid any contractors that asks for cash only, pressures you to make a quick decision, or seems sketchy to you in anyway. Trust your gut and don't hesitate to look elsewhere if you have any doubts about their integrity.

Contacting the Contractor:

Now that you have a list of potential contractors for the job, you can begin looking at their credentials. Begin with their website. You can use certifications to narrow down your search.

Some of the certifications contractors hold are from professional associations like National Association of the Remodeling Industry (NARI), National Association of Home Builders (NAHB) or National Kitchen and Bath Association (NKBA).

When you call them make sure you have your list with the ability to take notes that you can reference later. Let them know the scope and budget of what you are planning and ask them if they do work in that scope and if they have any scheduling constraints that would prevent them from starting the job within the time table you are hoping for. Make sure to ask how long they have been in business and how do they usually plan and execute work for projects such as yours.

Pay close attention to the questions they are asking you, as this might be a good indicator of how well they will listen to you and try to understand your needs and goal with the project.

Ask the contractor if they will provide references and if it would be possible for you to see some of their previous work or any jobs they are currently working on.

When they provide references make sure to call them and ask them necessary questions that will help you understand the quality, customer service, and work processes the company uses to complete the project. Ask them if they are satisfied with the work and would they recommend the contractor to friends and family. Ask them if anything went wrong and how that was handled.

If you are satisfied with this initial interview make a note in your list. Any contractors that do not meet your requirements or you don't want to work with for any reason will be removed or scratched off your list.

Now you will have a shorter list of contractors that you would like to meet with. Take this shortened list and call the contractors back to schedule an appointment to meet them at their office or have them come to your home to see the potential job site. If you are working with a designer, make sure that you will have the design or at least a rough design done so the contractor can understand the scope of work and answer your questions more easily.

Meet your contractor and ask them both generic as well as specific questions related to your project. Take good notes or just take a recording device of some type so that you can have a record that you can refer to later when making notes about the meeting or reviewing to decide on the contractor you hope to work with.

Also, pay attention to how well they listen, the questions they ask you, and all other aspects of how well you both communicate with each other.

Ask to see any certifications, licenses or other such things at this time.

Ask to see pictures of previous jobs they have completed. Discuss the budget and scope of your project and ask about materials, upgrades and design considerations.

At this point if you are comfortable and you think they are a great contractor, ask for a bid on your remodeling project. The more detailed the better. Make sure the bid includes and estimated project and payment schedule.

Get at least three bids, although more is certainly acceptable. Review them all and see if they are apples to apples. Look for differences in materials and key words like all wood, instead of solid wood (it is definitely not the same). Just give it a really good look to make sure they have everything accounted for and that the things listed are comparable. If they include brand names go onto the internet and research that brand name to check on quality, value, and read any reviews. If you find you have any questions as a result of your research or looking at the bids, call the contractor and ask. They should be happy to answer them for you.

Now you have met and interviewed the contractors, checked the references, checked company reviews, received detailed bids, reviewed the bids, conducted research and gotten all your questions answered. It is time to pick a contractor to do the work. You will have to decide what is important to you about your job and the contractor you pick. You might make the decision on price, or what references said, or customer service awards, or perhaps you just connected with one and you had a good feeling about the company. At this point, don't stress too much about your choice. If you have done the pre-work, then whoever you pick should be a rock star contractor that will do a fantastic job for you.

The contractor will provide you with a finalized estimate and a contract. The contract may be part of the estimate or not.

The contract should include the following:

- A complete project timeline. It may just be estimates, but it is good to know when they propose to stop and how long they think the project will last.

- Information on how any changes to the scope of work are handled, communicated, approved, and paid for.

- Information about permits and permissions required and who will be responsible for obtaining them. (This should always be the contractor or one of the subcontractors)

- Project description in detail including materials to be used as well as brand of fixtures and appliances.

- Proof of insurance coverage and damage liability.

- The approved payment schedule and what triggers each payment.

- Any special terms and conditions which may be applicable to your remodeling project.

Once you have a contract in hand take time to read it well and consult with anybody who may have experience with contracts. Sign on the dotted line only when all your questions are answered and you are satisfied with the contract.

Now that you have your contract signed you are well on your way to your dream kitchen.

Chapter 7: Working With Your Contractor

Congratulations! You have made your choice and the real adventure is about to begin. The next step is figuring out how to work with your contractor during the construction period to ensure a safe, high quality, low stress job is done, and that all your expectations are met.

Open lines of communication

Now usually there will be two scenarios when you have a contractor working in your home. Scenario one is everyone in the house works during the day and can't take time off work to be home while the work is being done. The second scenario is that someone is at home during the day and will be there during the duration of the work.

For those of us that work during the day and can't be on site for the remodel there are many things to consider. What is the best way to communicate if the contractor or one of the subcontractors has questions for you, or vice versa. Some of the things that need to be decided are: how will access to and from your house be granted. Will you give someone a set of keys to the house or will there be some kind of lockbox? Will the contractor have someone in the house when subcontractors are there? Can you stop by each day and check with workman who are there? What valuables or fragile pieces need to be put somewhere safe (I suggest all of them), and what areas of the house will be off limits? This last question might be important if you are keeping pets there while people are in and out of your house or for any other reason.

If you can't be onsite during the day make it a routine to meet the contractor or the person in charge of the job site before you leave for work. Take stock of work done and the schedule for the day. Make note of what the contractor says he expects to complete that day. This way if you have any concerns or spot something you can bring it to the contractors notice right away.

Ensure you have the contractor and foremen's cellphone number and in turn share your best contact number with them. Ask them for permission to call them in the course of the day to check on the work done. You can use your lunch break to call the contractor or even visit your home if possible. This will keep the contractor and his crew alert because they will anticipate surprise checks.

If you can, try to be there at end of the workday to ensure everything that was promised was done.

Some homeowners find it easy to keep track of things by using a journal to organize their thoughts. Jot down notes and questions that you might have. Maintaining a journal, taking lots of pictures or video also ensures there is a clear record to refer to in case of a dispute.

If there are any changes to be done which will add to the cost of the project ensure you get it in writing from the contractor and sign it to signify your approval.

Ask for Work Schedule

Make sure your contractor provides a work schedule before project begins. It will contain number of days required for project and break down of work allocated for the day. This may change during the project if problems arise during the remodel. This will help you understand the work flow of the project and give you definite times certain upgrade or change decisions have to be made.

Having an idea of the work flow schedule will allow you to be prepared. You will have an idea of when the tearout will happen, when the flooring will be done (which means no walking in this area!), etc. The more you know, the easier it will be to coordinate around the work area, especially if you have a young family.

This will also help you know when to you will need to release milestone payments on scheduled completion of work. We assume that you have already prepared and agreed upon a payment schedule while drawing out the contract for the project.

Discuss preparations which need to be done

Discuss all preparations that need to be done in your home before work begins. This may involve moving things to a different room to free up work space. You may also need to cover appliances and carpets so that they do not get dirty from all the construction debris.

Discuss with you contractor who moves what as far as furniture and appliances, and who put them back or reinstalls them after the work is complete. It is important to get this in writing or even better yet make sure it is in the contract.

Pack all fragile belongings in and around the work area beforehand to ensure they are safe. Failing to do so may lead to heartbreak later. Even workers being as careful as possible may accidentally bump that wall hanging maneuvering with large cabinets in boxes.

Be Proactive

Do not adopt the "in our contractor we trust" approach. Be proactive when you are home and check all the work that is being done. If you are there during the day, regularly inspect to make sure quality work is being done and that everything is being completed to your satisfaction. Ask questions and if they are not doing things that are expected or agreed upon, bring it up with the contractors foreman or job lead as quickly as you can.

Check model numbers and tally them with receipts/invoice to ensure that the contractor is using the same brand and model of appliances or fixtures which was agreed upon.

Keep good notes in your journal and take good pictures or video. If you cannot be home during the remodel each day, you will have to do this each evening when you get home. Be sure to make note of it in the journal at that time or you may forget to bring it up in the morning when you meet with the contractor.

Don't be shy, you are paying them for a quality job and it is your responsibility to make sure that is exactly what you get. Sure you hired a rock star contractor, but that doesn't mean you shouldn't be paying attention. It is a great idea to take pictures all along the process. The pictures become a great way to share the transformation taking place in your home as well as record details in case anything comes up later that needs to be addressed.

Be a Good Client

The best way to get good work done from your contractor and crew is to be nice to them. Do not act like a dictator, be courteous but firm.

Make it a point to know the names of the people on the construction crew and refer to them by their name. Greet them each morning and ask them how they are doing before you begin talking about the project.

If they have done good work appreciate their efforts. If there are things that need improvement, share constructive feedback in a polite and courteous way.

Designate a bathroom they can use and show them where it is. Make sure it is properly stocked with toilet paper, soap and a towel. It is also polite to make sure they have access to drinking water as they work hard all day. They usually carry all of their own refreshments with them but the offer will make them feel important and welcome in your home. Welcome employees are much harder workers than those who feel uncomfortable at work.

The crew will most likely leave for their lunch break, but if not, it is nice to let them know where they can sit and relax in your home as they eat their lunch. As your kitchen will not be functioning... showing them a table and chairs on the patio in good weather is a great touch. Or even a small card table and chairs off to the side in your construction area will be appreciated by the workers. After all, you and your family will want a place to sit and eat as well so why not share this luxury with the people making your dream kitchen come to life.

Dealing with Workmen in your home

You know your contractor and trust them, however you have no control over the choice of workmen in your home. Although the contractor and his employees are most likely fantastic, safe and trustworthy, stuff happens. Not only will the contractor's employees be in your home, there will be sub-contractors and delivery drivers there as well. Not everyone can be watched every minute of every day.

Therefore, make sure all workers understand the house rules and areas of the house where they are not allowed. For example, sometimes workers are smokers and you are not, in fact lets suppose you really hate the smell of cigarette smoke.

The workers would never smoke in your house, but they may need to step outside to smoke during their breaks. The least stressful way to deal with it if you are a nonsmoker is to designate a place workers can smoke if they need to. Put a coffee can for cigarette butts in a corner of your backyard...or out by the sidewalk in front of your home if that makes you more comfortable. Planning ahead for this will help everyone involved avoid unnecessary conflict and stress. This is a much more positive approach than getting upset after the fact when a worker stubs out a cigarette on your driveway and tosses the butt in your trashcan.

When all of these different workers, delivery drivers and supervisors are coming in and out of your home, it is a good idea to remove valuables from the area. Generally, workers are honest and you will have no concerns, however, there are occasionally exceptions. To remove temptation you can place valuables in a room, such as a bedroom, that can be locked during the day. Of course, most bedroom locks are designed to keep out serious thieves, but just having the items out of site is generally all you need to do.

Construction work is messy and it can be upsetting to come home after long day at work and have to clean up after the construction crew. If the contractor or his subcontractors are not adequately cleaning up after work each day or leaving the house in an unsafe manner, speak to the contractor and share your concerns.

Showing them where they can dispose of their own personal trash such as cans and sandwich wrappers can also help them keep their work area clean. Obviously, they usually cannot dispose of all of their daily construction trash in your waste containers, but it will help keep the area clean if they don't have to wait for a construction trash container haul to get rid of their lunch trash.

Pets and Construction

If you have pets you will need to make special arrangements for them. Even if your pets are friendly, you will want to keep them out of the way of the workmen. Remember, doors will be open a lot to bring items in and out, you don't want workers to have to watch for escaping pets while they are carrying heavy loads in and out of your home.

The safest thing for your pets is to confine them away from the construction area during the day. Even caged animals should be moved out of the work area. Some birds, reptiles and even fish can be sensitive to the chemicals used in painting or striping floors, walls and cabinets. No matter what the pet, it is a good idea to get them away from the construction area before the project begins.

Cats are easier than dogs when it comes to this. Put them in a room, like the bathroom or a bedroom, away from where the construction is taking place. Bring their food, water and litterbox in the room for them and they should be fine all day while the workers are there. Most cats spend a lot of their time sleeping anyway so after a little bit they will give up crying to be let out and just take a catnap.

Dogs are not always so easy to confine if they are not used to it. If the weather is good and the construction workers do not need access to your backyard, you can put them outside in a fenced yard while workmen are there. Make sure they have their normal food and water available during this time.

If your dog is not used to being outside alone all day, he may bark and disturb the neighbors though. This is especially common because he wants to alert you to the presence of strangers in his house. Don't scold him for this, it is his job to protect his property and his family. He is just trying to do what he thinks he should.

For many dogs, this barking will be greatly reduced if they are introduced to the people working in your home. It is best to do this with the dog on a leash, even a small dog, as sometimes dogs do bite in these stressful situations. This is true for even the best family dog so don't take any chances. Not only will you have an injured workman and a delay in construction, you and your dog could have negative consequences if the bite is reported to authorities who may be required by law to quarantine the animal afterward in case of rabies or other illness.

Sometimes the safest option for your dog in this type of situation, especially if you cannot be home during the day, is to kennel them. If you do not have a kennel at home, you can often find a boarding facility close to you that will take them during the day while you are at work. Or, maybe you have a friend or family member that the pet is comfortable with that will take the dog during the day for you.

Confining dogs to a room in your house by itself while workers are there isn't always a good idea. Dogs can become very upset by the closed door and all of the activity taking place on the other side of the door. In addition to barking a lot, the dog may scratch at the door and flooring in front of the door. Even a very small dog can do significant damage to flooring and wood over the course of several hours.

Because you know your pets better than anyone, it will be up to you to choose the best option to keep everyone and everything safe during construction. Plan ahead and even give your plan a trial run a few days before the work crews start to get the animals used to the situation.

Planning ahead will save you and your family a lot of stress with regards to your pets during construction. Pets are important part of our family and keeping them safe should be a priority. It is an unnecessary heartbreak if a pet becomes lost or injured when it escapes out the front door while workman are hauling in their materials.

Keep pets and workers safe by restricting your pet's access to the area of the house where they are working. Not only are they in the way, but they risk injury if they are underfoot.

What to do if there are problems?

Make sure to pay attention to the quality of work being done and that the right materials, fixtures, and appliances are being installed. If you notice poor quality workmanship, or anything else wrong it is your responsibility to inform the contractor.

Depending on what it is, you may or may not want to bring it up with the workman, but you certainly want to bring it up with the foreman or contractors representative as quickly as possible. Make sure to be polite and non-confrontational during the discussion.

Consider this scenario: The tile subcontractor is using the wrong tile or doing a subpar job on installation. You may want to tell the tile subcontractor they are using the wrong tile and feel comfortable with that. On the other hand you may not want to tell the subcontractor they are doing a crappy job on the installation, but you will want to tell the contractor immediately that the work is not acceptable quality. That way they can address it right away saving both time and schedule.

Issues like this you want to address immediately or as close to immediately as possible. These are not things you want to just put on a list to be addressed at the end of the job because by then it might be too late or extremely expensive and time consuming to fix or change.

Chapter 8: Preparing for Construction

The budget is set, the new vision has been designed, a rock start contractor has been hired, materials were ordered, now the fun begins. Get ready to accept the fact that for a few weeks your kitchen will be a disaster. It will all be worth it though because at the end of these few short weeks you will have an amazing new space in your home to enjoy with your family and friends.

Before you start to pack up your kitchen, it is time to plan how you will feed your family while the kitchen is out of commission. I know everyone thinks it is wonderful to have to eat out for several weeks, the reality is this is expensive and can be tiring. You really don't need to eat out for this whole time.

Plan where your refrigerator will go during construction. Get an inexpensive piece of plywood at your local do it yourself store and have it cut to just a little larger than the base of your refrigerator. Lay this down on carpet and you will be able to place your refrigerator on it without damaging your carpet. Choose a place convenient but not too far from the kitchen since stocked refrigerators are a little difficult to move. The best option is to have it fairly empty because things can tip over, spill and break in transit. It is important that you keep the appliance as upright as possible when moving it. After you have it where you want for the next few weeks, plug the refrigerator back in.

Even if you are keeping existing stove / range, you will probably not be able to easily use these during construction. A great cooking option is a crock pot or electric frying pan. A microwave can also be placed in a useable location to enable you to reheat previously prepared meals. At the end of this book are several recipes you can prepare using a crockpot or electric frypan that are healthy and delicious. There are many more available on the internet as well.

When using these appliances outside your kitchen, be careful you do not damage the surface you set them on. You can place a large cutting board, hot pads or other protective layer between the appliance and your furniture if it is wood, laminate or other product which heat can damage.

One place that might work well to set up a small temporary kitchen is your laundry room. There is usually an electrical outlet handy and the surface of the washer and dryer are impervious to the heat of your crockpot and electric frying pan. Remember to remove these appliances before running the washer or dryer since movement of the appliance if the load becomes off balanced will cause your appliance to shift and it could fall to the ground and break.

Using a folding table is another great way to set up a temporary kitchen off to the side of a room. To protect carpet underneath this cooking area, spread a tarp or inexpensive disposable tablecloth. Place your crockpot, electric frying pan, rice cooker, microwave or coffeepot on this table. You can use the space underneath the table to store the appliances you are not using but need easy access to them. Remember if you are using only one electrical outlet you won't want to run more than two of these at a time or you may trip your breaker.

Make it easy on yourself and use paper plates and plastic utensils during construction. Cooking without a kitchen is not as hard as you think if you plan ahead, but doing dishes too starts to make you feel like you are camping in your own home. There are better things to spend your time on so go ahead and use paper plates. Put some foods your family can "grab and go" handy. Things like fresh fruit in a bowl and granola bars can be a great quick and healthy snack for you and your family.

For breakfast, cereal, bagels, fruit and yoghurt are great options. You don't need to do any cooking for these quick and inexpensive breakfasts. Lunch, if you are home or even if you are packing to go, can be sandwiches, precut and prepared veggie sticks and fresh fruit are all easy to make. All you need is access to your refrigerator and a clean flat surface to do sandwich assembly. No kitchen, no problem.

Dinner can be a little more challenging but you will be surprised how easy and healthy it can be. Crockpot meals are great meal options. For example, you can put a pot roast, a bag of already washed baby carrots, a package of frozen green beans, and a couple of cut and washed potatoes into the crockpot in the morning with some garlic, black pepper and salt. Then, at dinnertime you have a filling, easy cleanup meal ready for your family. Serve it with a simple premade bagged Caesar salad and some fresh baked bread from the grocery store.

With a rice cooker and an electric frying pan you can make healthy stir fry meals in minutes. Place your rice in the rice cooker. Heat up the electric frying pan. For meat, your local grocery store will usually offer thin sliced chicken, often advertised for fajitas or stir fry. You could use pork or beef too if you prefer. Put the meat and a big bag of frozen veggies into the frying pan coated with a little oil. Cover and cook, stirring frequently. When veggies have defrosted, add your favorite Asian sauce, such as teriyaki. Continue cooking and stirring until meat and veggies are cooked through. This usually takes about 15 to 20 minutes. Serve over the rice you made in the rice cooker for a quick and healthy meal that everyone will love.

Meals like this take a lot less time and are far less expensive than going to a restaurant every night while your kitchen is undergoing its renovation. They are also far healthier than those fast food options too. When you plan ahead and have a place set up to do your meal preparation being without your kitchen for a couple of weeks will not be nearly as stressful as you think.

If the weather cooperates, you can plan to cook some of your meals outside by utilizing your BBQ or camping stove if you have them. It would be terrific if you created a remodel meal plan so you knew each night what you were going to prepare and how. That way you could make some things a head of time and then take them out and warm them up, some things on the BBQ both meat and veggies, and maybe some "one pot" meals that can be prepared on a hot plate or outside on a camp stove. It would help make preparing meals during the remodel less stressful and more like a fun adventure for the family.

Even if you are just having your cabinets refaced, not replaced, you will probably still need to empty all of the cabinets. Weeks before construction begins, start collecting boxes to do this. Newspaper can protect your packed dishes, but bubble wrap and even cloth napkins or small towels work well too. Depending on who you know or where you work you may be able to get free packing materials by asking friends, family and coworkers to save any shipping materials they get in their packages. You won't have to pack as well as you would for a move across town, but make sure you protect the breakables because you will need to move the boxes out of the kitchen area.

As a precaution, some people will cover their furniture with drop cloths. Your construction crew can let you know what areas they recommend you cover and what furniture, knickknacks or decorative items they want you to move before they come to start the project.

A good construction crew will take every precaution to protect your flooring, walls and furniture. They will cover high traffic areas if necessary. Discuss any concerns you have with extra wear and tear on your carpet or lawn with them before they arrive.

The crew will probably need a work area where they can do final detailed cuts or preparation. A garage space works great as an all weather work space, but your driveway, patio or even lawn may work as well. Before work starts discuss what area you will allow them to set up. Work crew should leave the work area neat at the end of the day, but keep in mind some projects will require their tools multiple days so they may prefer to leave their saws, etc set up overnight.

If the crew will be working in an area where your lawn sprinklers go off, adjust the schedule so that your work crew and their tools do not get wet in an unexpected shower. You can set the sprinklers to go off at night after they have cleaned up and left for the day or, if they are leaving items out in the yard, turn them off for a couple of days. The crew will not be happy if their work area is wet when they arrive to work or if the tools and materials they leave in your yard get soaked overnight. Of course, if there is rain predicted the crew should arrange to protect their equipment before they leave for the day.

If you have children or pets, you will need to be extra vigilant to keep them out of harms way. During this project your home will no longer be childproofed and no matter how clean the workers leave the area, there will be things that you may not want your children to touch in the construction area. Before the project starts explain to the children why they need to stay out of the construction area. To encourage them to stay away, show them where their snacks or other items usually stored in the kitchen will be. Then they have no reason to go into the construction area.

Pets who have been locked up all day while the workers were in the house may be a little more excited and active at night. Taking them for a walk will help them burn up this energy so they sleep better. Otherwise, if they slept all day, they may be up much later at night and looking for more attention than usual. Dogs and cats will want to smell the areas where the strangers have been in there house. This is normal and as long as they aren't in danger of stepping on or knocking over anything that could hurt them there is no reason not to let them take in the new smells.

At the end of each construction day, the workers should put items away and clean up the area. If they aren't doing this, talk to the supervisor and ask that they do this before they leave. Cleaning up the area does NOT mean that all of their items will be put away....it means there is not trash or cut scraps and nails laying all over the floor. Cleaning up also means that the tools are placed out of the way instead of scattered across the walkways. They won't take out all of the tools being used for multiple days. Think if this as a timesaver, which means they can spend more time each day transforming your kitchen instead of setting up and tearing down the tools.

I cannot stress enough the safety reasons for keeping your children out of the construction area, both when the workmen are there and at night. Toddlers and other young children need to be watched very diligently because their natural curiosity will lead them to investigate all of the new items they see in their home. Older children usually understand the danger of situations better so it is easier to explain to them why they need to stay out of the area.

Set up an area away from the construction where you and your kids can hang out, play games and do homework. For younger kids, usually out of sight is out of mind so they will quickly forget all about the chaos of the other room if they cannot see it.

Give your older children a tour of the construction area if they are interested in the project. Explain what is happening in language they can understand. They will be less likely to go off exploring on their own if they have an opportunity to do it with you.

Above all, try and relax and enjoy the transformation taking place in your home. Don't stress over a little dust or disorganization. If it is really bothering you, retreat to an area of the house unaffected by the construction, like your bedroom. Or, take an opportunity to enjoy a local park or a movie in the evening with your family instead of sitting at home in the mess. The dust and mess will clean up easier than you think in the end and no point in cleaning and dusting more than once if you can hold out just a few more days.

Also, don't forget to keep taking those photographs, especially the before and after ones. The photographs are fun to look at when the project is over. They are also a good way to document anything you need to remember, like where the new electrical lines for the under cabinet light run through the wall. You will want to know this in case you have a problem someday down the road!

Chapter 9: Post Job Inspection

Since we spent time finding a great contractor and were well prepared for construction, it is time to sit back, relax and let the construction crew work its magic.

All that is left to do is to inspect the work done after it is completed.
As mentioned earlier you need to take a lot of pictures, maintain a journal and keep an eye on the day to day progress of the project.

Once the construction is complete everything should be to your satisfaction and according to what was agreed in the contract. If you are not happy with the work or feel quality has been compromised you need to speak up now or forever hold your peace.

Make sure every area of the home is cleared and cleaned up. The work crews should clean up all of their tools, trash and scraps both in the kitchen and in the area where they have been making their trims and using their other tools outside. You should not have to haul away the construction trash unless this was something you arranged in the contract.

For example, if your old cabinets or countertops come out of your kitchen in good shape, you might consider donating them to a local contractor like Habitat for Humanity. Your contractor will probably not make these arrangements but it doesn't hurt to ask if they do.

Or, maybe you want to install those old kitchen cabinets in your garage for additional storage space. You can either have the contractor leave the cabinets and you can do it yourself, or you can see if you can arrange something with the installers to do this for you.

When you do the final walk through with the contractor make sure you get all of the manuals and care instructions on your new appliances, sinks, faucets, garbage disposal and anything else that was installed new. Test all of the appliances to make sure they are working as well.

Open and close all of the cabinets and drawers to make sure they are operating properly and are not rubbing on other surfaces when you open them. This is the time to pay special attention to surfaces for scratches, nicks or other damage that may need to be repaired. Finding it now means the contractor will do his best to fix it because it was probably caused during installation. If you come back a week or two later with these types of repairs they might not be so willing to fix them at no charge because they could have easily happened when you were putting your kitchen cabinets back together, which makes the repairs your fault, not theirs.

Ask the contractor on tips for maintenance of countertops and other materials in your new kitchen. Be aware that although granite and other hard surfaces are extremely strong, using the wrong product on them can damage them. For example, natural stone is affected by very acidic cleaners, such as those with lemon in them like the popular Pine Sol cleaner. Ask what recommended cleaning and care products you should use. They will know both the names of the expensive products you can buy, but they will probably also have some great day to day tips that are less expensive and will keep your surfaces looking beautiful every day.

When doing the walk through with the contractor, make a list of anything that needs to be fixed or finished. Make sure both of you have a copy of the same list. Do not release final payment until these repairs are made to your satisfaction.

Remember, a complete kitchen remodel is a huge project, sometimes not everything goes smoothly. For example, maybe the door pulls you ordered were shipped late by the manufacturer. This type of situation is out of your contractor's control. As long as he is doing everything he can to rectify the situation, getting aggressive or demanding isn't going to make it happen any faster. However, if you think the contractor is not making a genuine effort to fix a problem, you may need to be a little more firm. Give him a chance to fix it in a timely manner.

Once you are satisfied with the entire project on completion you can release the final payment.

If there have been cost overruns you would need to pay the difference. Explore possibility of the contractor offering you a discount because these costs were not part of original quote. If you have been working closely with your contractor and communicating there should be no big surprises when your final bill is presented.

If there are any big surprises on the bill, it is time for you and your contractor to sit down and work out the details. This is where all of your documentation, photographs and journal, will really come in handy. It is nice to pull out the information and find your notes on what you and the contractor discussed when you made the change to the kitchen plan which resulted in the overrun. Of course, any big change in prices should have been presented to you in writing before they completed the work if you have been communicating.

Generally contractors in good standing with their local better business bureau and who have good reviews from their customers have these for a reason. They communicate well with their customers and you shouldn't have any big surprises with billing or quality of their work. This is why the earlier due diligence is so important when finding, interviewing and hiring the contractor.

If you do have concerns that you cannot work out by sitting down with the contractor, you may have to take further action and meet with legal help. Hopefully it will never come to this. However, if you feel that the contractor is not holding up their end of the contract and you are making no progress maybe just a mediation appointment with legal help will be all you need to resolve the issues. Make sure you have everything documented before this appointment or it could be a waste of time and money since you will probably have to pay your lawyer if you win or lose.

Most contractors will ask you to provide feedback on their work once the project is complete. You can also leave feedback for the contractor on independent sites like Angie's List or Houzz.com. These reviews are some of the things you looked for and read before you hired him as a contractor so it is important that you leave your feedback for others looking to do the same.

Once that is all done and the dust has settled you can click an "after picture" of your kitchen and compare it to the old kitchen. If you enjoyed or found other people's before and after pictures helpful, you can share your experience as well. Provide your contractor with good before / after photographs too. It is fun to know that other people are getting to enjoy and be inspired by the beauty of your remodeled kitchen when they are looking for ideas for their own kitchen.

After everything is back together and you have had a chance to privately enjoy your new kitchen, a party to show off your kitchen is a lot of fun. Invite your friends and family over for the big "unveiling". This is a great time to display the photographs you took from start to finish. Who knows, you might inspire some of your friends to take on similar projects in their own home.

A FREE GIFT FOR YOU

To express my thanks for your purchase we would like to give you a free gift. Follow the link below and you can download a Week of Easy Dinner Recipes you can make with only a crockpot and an electric frying pan PLUS a list of critical questions you should ask your contractor before you hire him.

Go to the link below to receive your FREE forms
Click here for your FREE Forms.

We know these will be helpful to you in your quest for your dream kitchen!
Thank you!
Kyle and Sandra McNatt

Made in the USA
San Bernardino, CA
13 May 2016